A BROAD on t
BOUNDARY
or
How I Fell in Love With the Game of Cricket
by
Linda Combi

FOURTH ESTATE - LONDON

First Published in Great Britain by
Fourth Estate Ltd.
289 Westbourne Grove
London W11 2QA

ISBN 1 85702 0928

Printed in Great Britain

To B.J. with Thanks —

HOW IT ALL STARTED....

1.

LUST

Led to the Desire to..

2.

LEARN
THE
RUDIMENTS

Thereby Resulting in a.

3.

DEEPER UNDERSTANDING

of the Noble Game.

A FRIENDLY PITCH

The NEW BALL **IS.......**

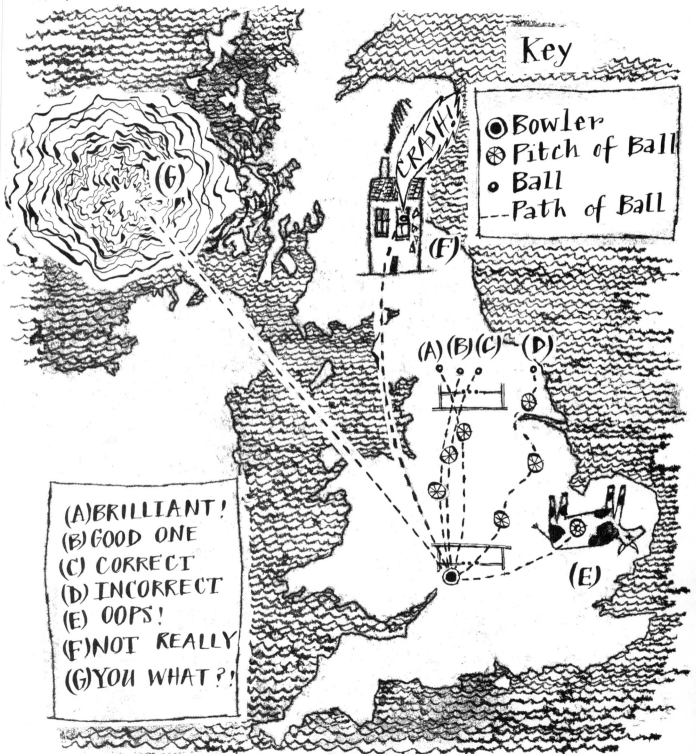

The Unpredictable Effects On A Ball When Pitched Into The Rough Created By Footmarks

The Theory of SWING....

ZE SVEORY OFF SVINK—

SHINY
POLISHED
SIDE

SEPARATION OF BOUNDARY AIR LAYER

INITIAL DIRECTION
OF BALL

RELATIVE HIGH PRESSURE

SEAM

LOW PRESSURE WAKE
RELATIVE LOW PRESSURE

ACTUAL LINE
OF SWING IS
RESULTANT OF
FORWARD AND
SIDEWAYS FORCE

SEPARATION

ROUGH
SIDE

SIDEWAYS FORCE CAUSED
BY UNEQUAL
PRESSURES BEHIND BALL

The INTRICACIES of BOWLING

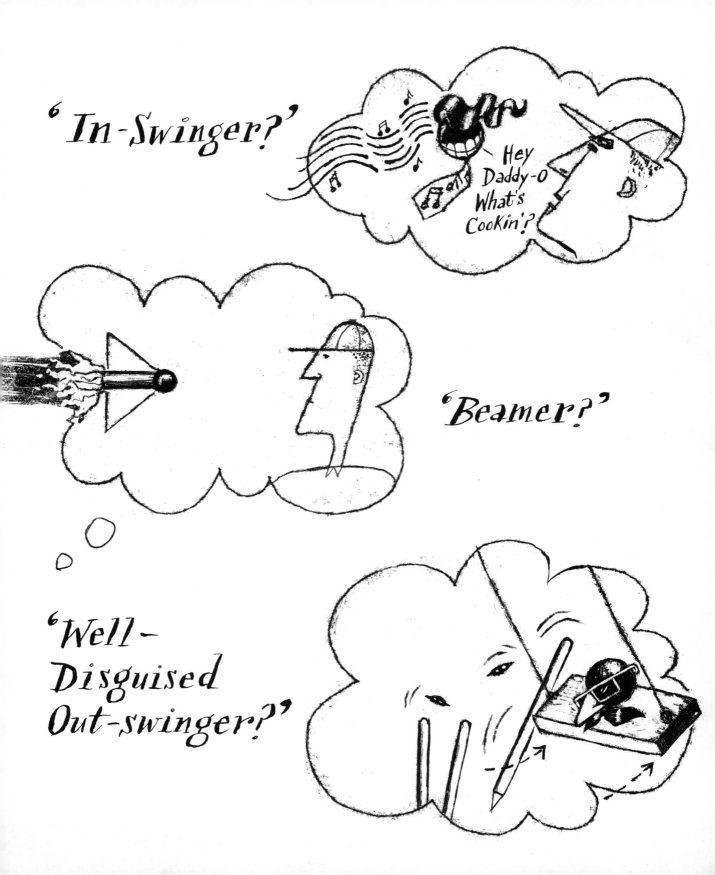

SOME BOWLING PROBLEMS:

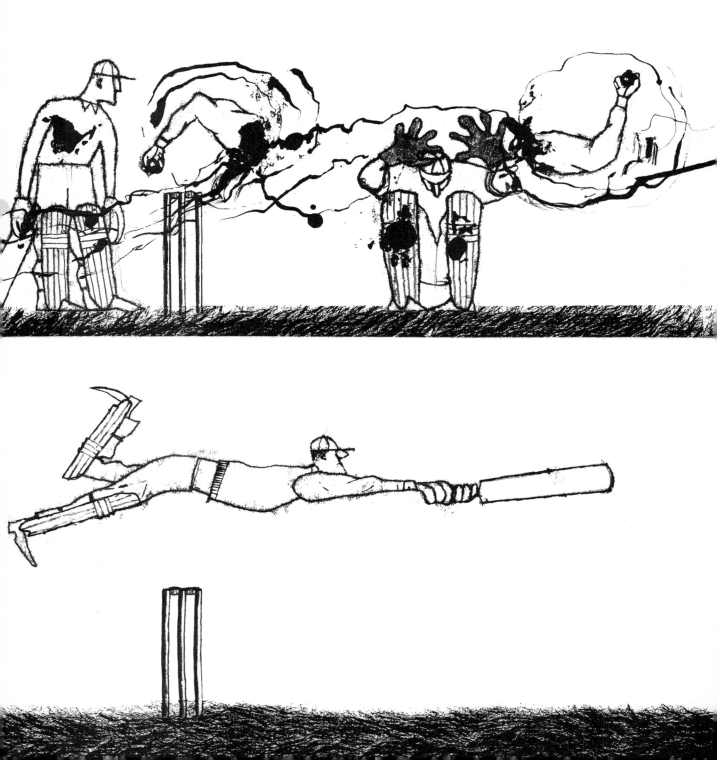

W----i----d----e

A Magnificent Example of Getting Behind a Fast, Rising Ball....

DEALING with ASIAN GUILE

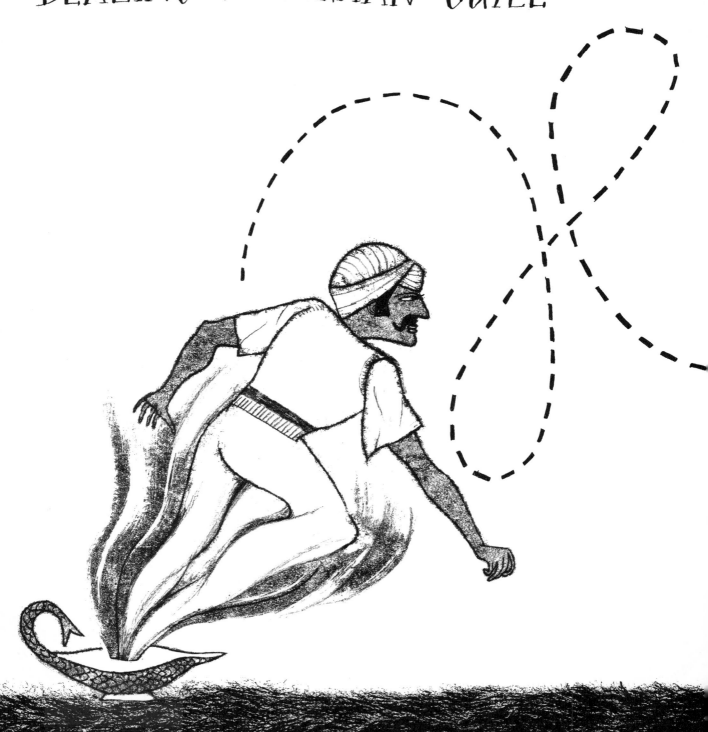

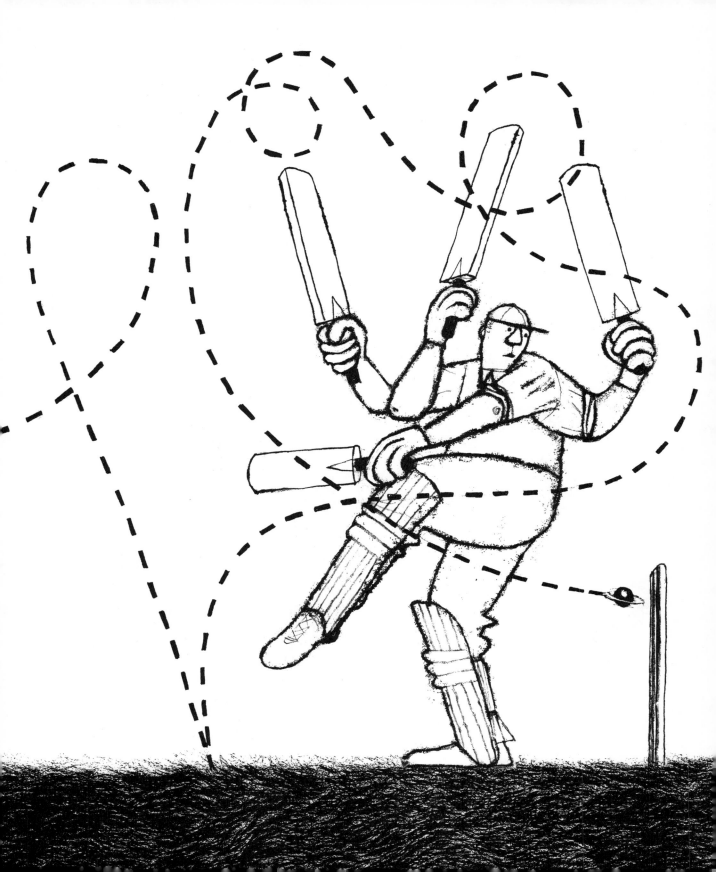

BATTING: RULE No 1 ~
Keep a Straight Bat!

Yes

No

BATTING HIERARCHY:
A Visual Metaphor~

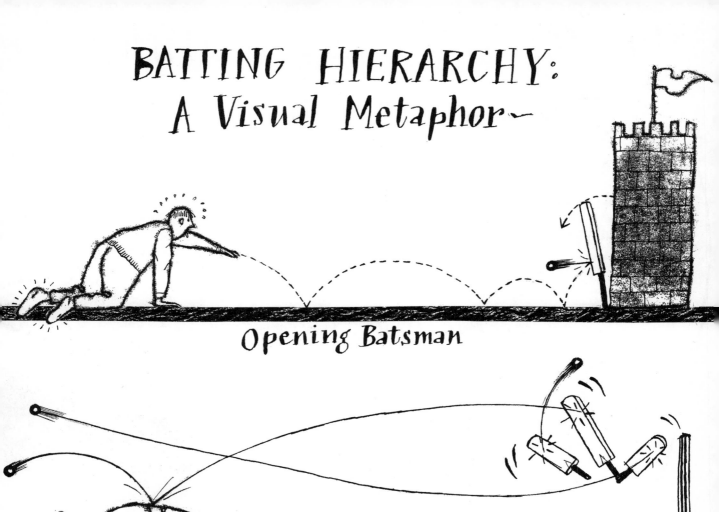

Opening Batsman

Middle Order Batsman

Lower Order Batsman

THE MYSTERIES of BATTING

THWOCK!

BATTING: There Are Several Ways One Can Be Out~

Handling the Ball:

RUN-OUT: A Misunderstanding   Mid-Wicket:

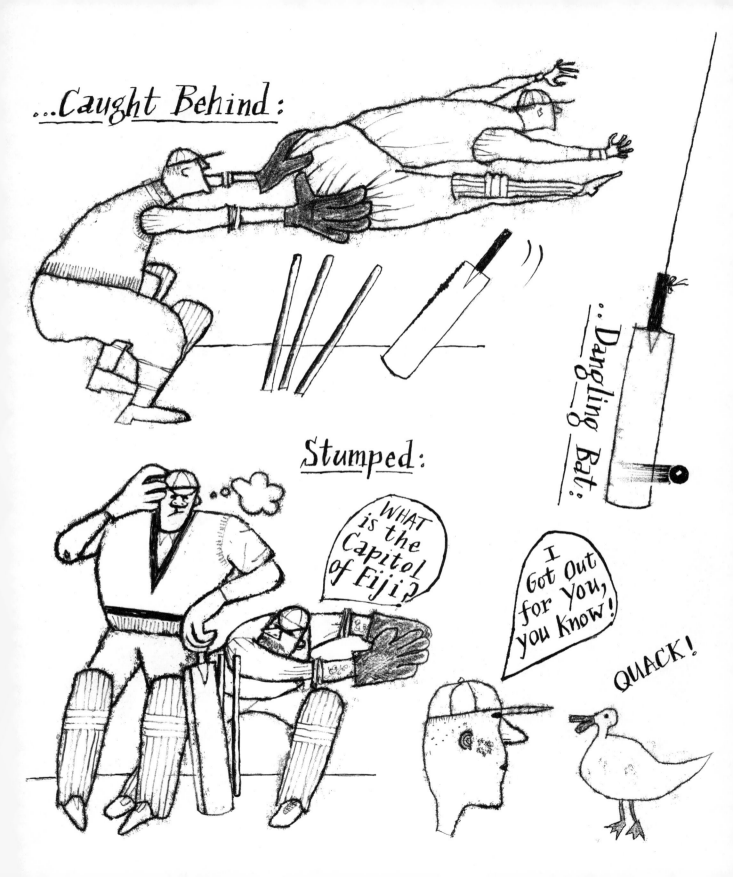

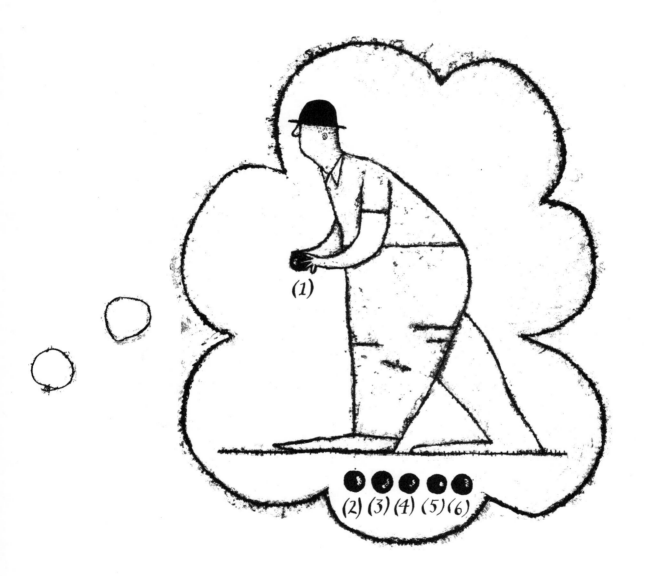

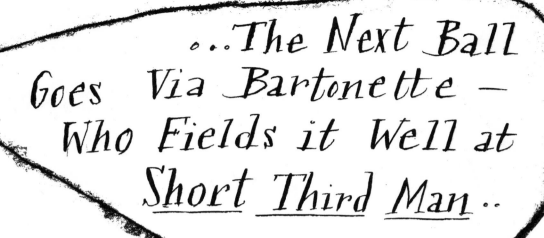

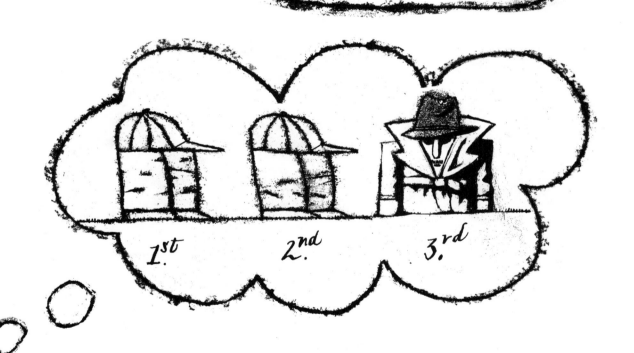

DIFFICULT CATCHES: The Skier

WICKETKEEPERS – Do:

1.) Let the Ball Come to You & Ride With it
(See Also: Rise With the Ball & Not Before).

2.) Get Across Early to the Leg-Side

3.) Take the Ball Cleanly.

4.) Concentrate When Standing Up to the Wicket.

5.) Keep Agile for Good Balance & Footwork.

WICKETKEEPING: Common Faults~

1.) Excessive Head Movement.~
(See Also: Loss of Concentration)

2.) Hesitation in Going for Wide Balls.

3.) Unnecessary Use of Pads.

TWO KINDS of ALL-ROUNDER~

1.) I.M.A. Paragon

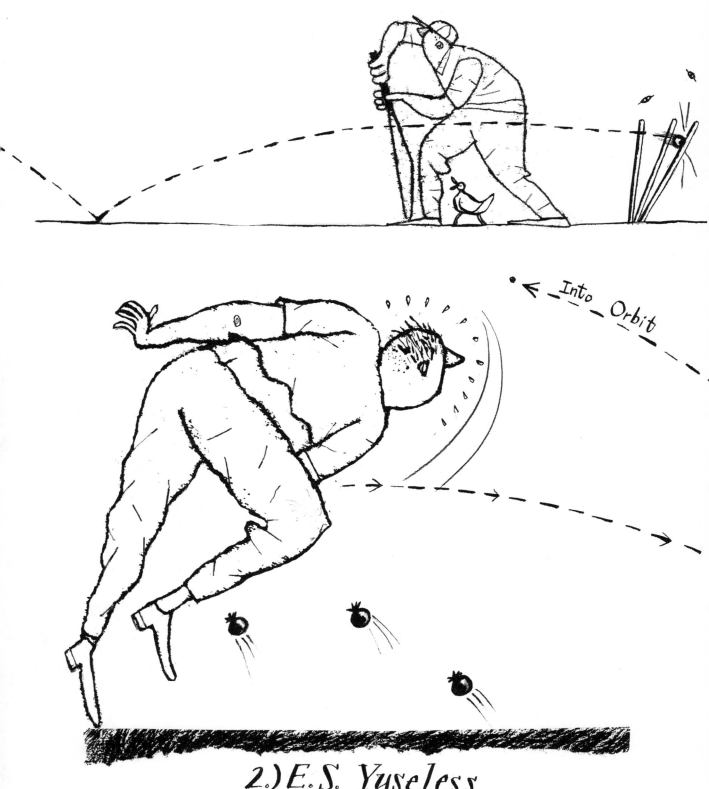

Into Orbit

2.) E.S. Yuseless

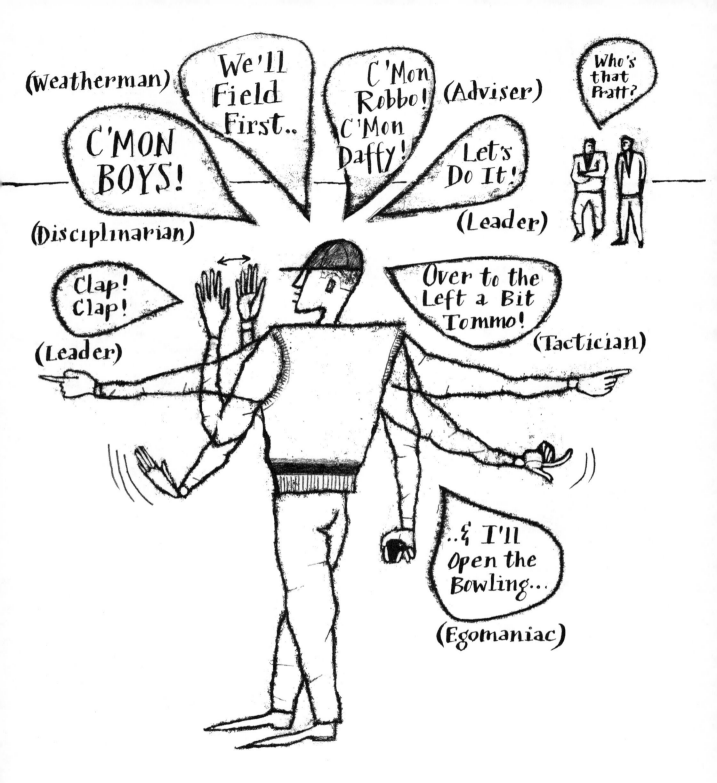

The Fielding Captain

DISTINCTIVE SIGNALS with 'Umpire Aids'

'Hats For Every Occasion'

Signal a 'Wide' in Comfort ‿

'No Ball' Hat ‿
Also Useful for:
'Call That Bowling?'

WALK!

Stubborn Batsman Won't Walk?
'The Cannon' doesn't Beat
About the Bush!

Tired Feet? Time for Lunch?
Whinge to the World with
the Adjustable 'Gripe-Alert'!

The UMPIRE CAN BE USEFUL AS A CLOTHESRACK~

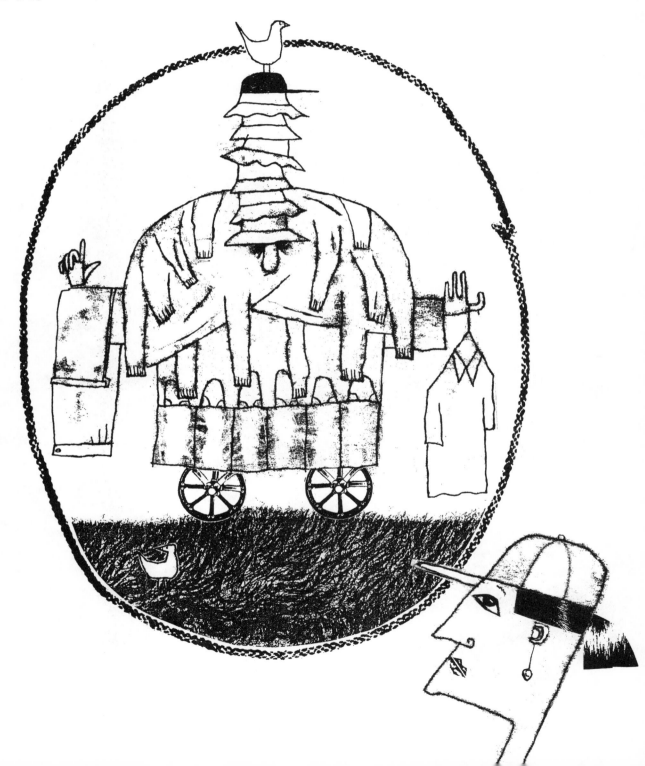

A DREAM ABOUT 'PYJAMA CRICKET...'

...And Thanks to Colonel Dozer for the Crate of Cocoa!

Cheers!

The ARRIVAL of YORKSHIRE'S FIRST OVERSEAS PLAYER

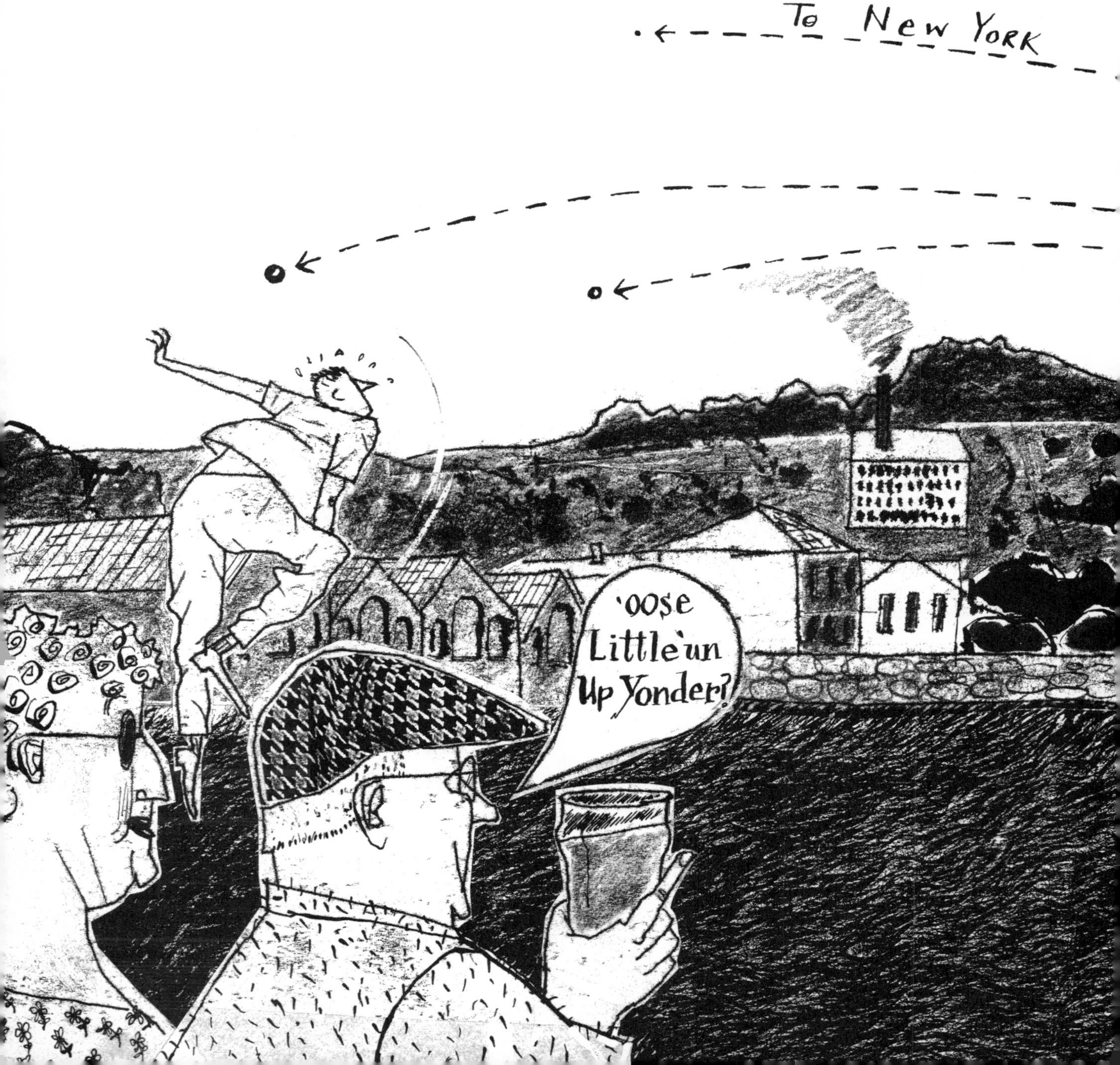

It is Essential That One Enters the Ground Through the Appropriate Gate...

Full Members

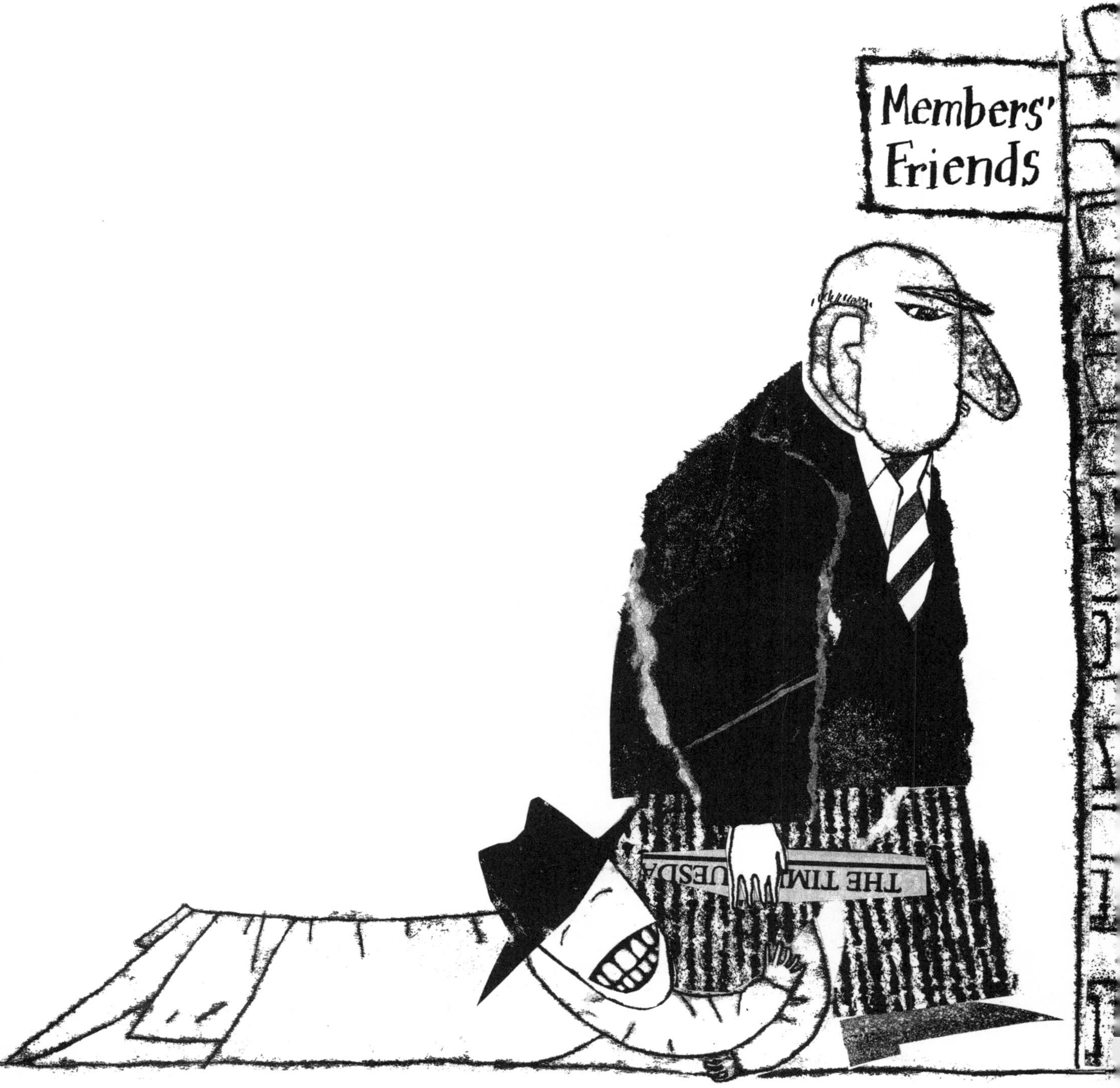
Members'
Friends

INGULUND INGULUND INGULUND INGULUND

b.) The Flower of English Manhood

c.) *Mrs. Tupperware*

'No Disrespect But:

I think **I** could've captained _____shire! He's not a genuinely fast bowler. He'll always be liable to back injury... I mean it's a 6* joke isn't it? The sad thing is, they get into the 6* 6* side & then they don't de- velop. He doesn't help himself, he doesn't know exactly where his off— is... If he'd left stump that, the other chap would've caught it... It was in the air a long time ~ 'Ees a 6* unlikely lookin' sportsman–Its the old adage – 'Catches Win Matches'! ~'Ees the main strike bowler now by necessity... Give Over! That's a Two!

d.) Our Expert

Lords: Post-Prandial Pavilion

A New Stand, Eden Gardens, Calcutta

The Winning Shot at Lahore

IT IS WISE TO COME PREPARED FOR THE FIRST MATCH OF THE SEASON~

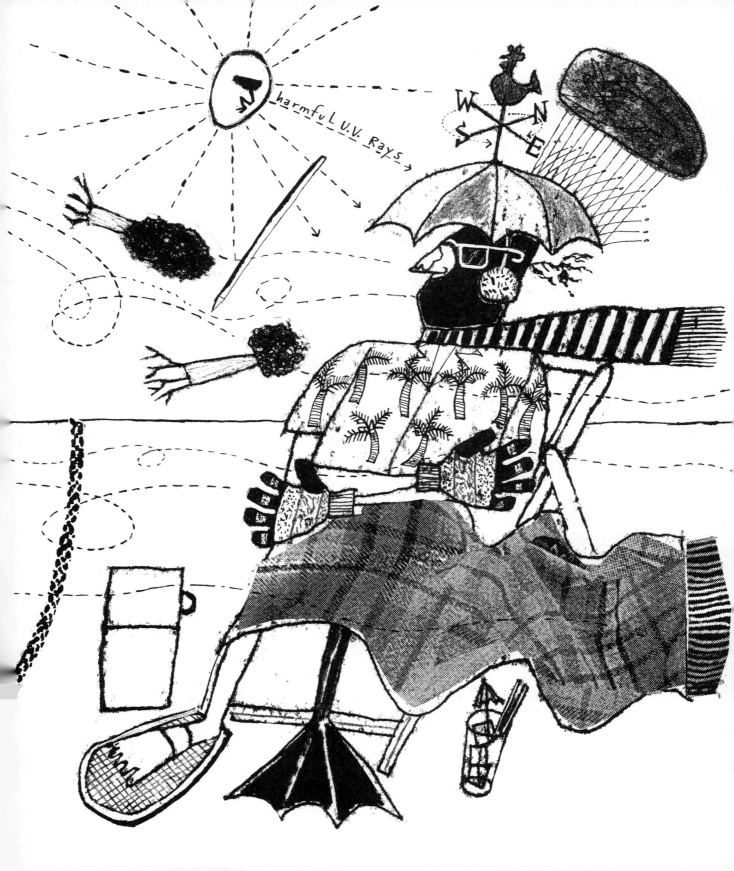

harmful U.V. Rays →

‘Ladies + Gentlemen; unfortunately, Rain has delayed the start of Play. The Umpires will make a Pitch Inspection in One Hour.....................’

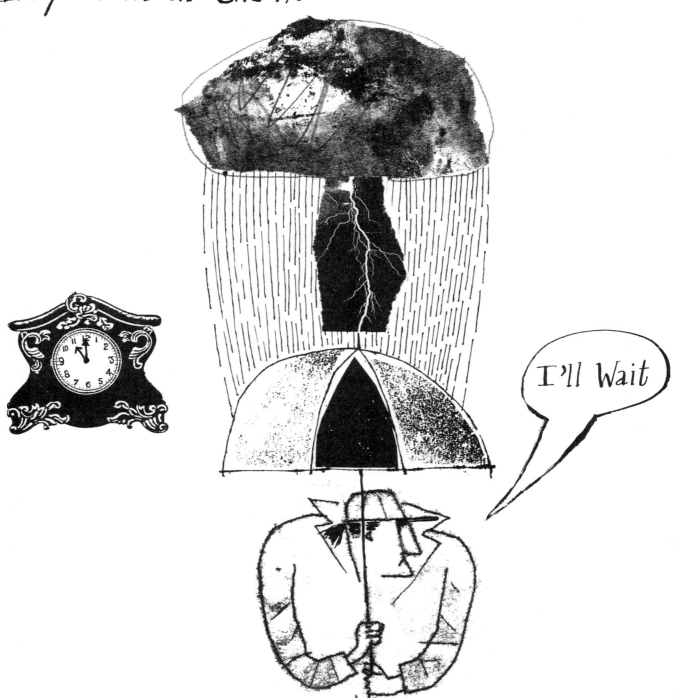

'Ladies + Gentlemen; it has Brightened up. Play will begin in One Hour. · · · · · · · · · · · · · · ·'

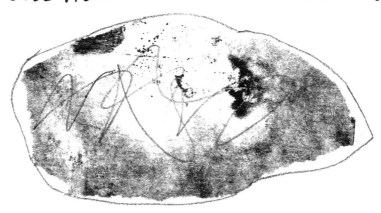

I'll Wait

'Ladies + Gentlemen; the Umpires will make an Inspection in One Hour. . . . .'

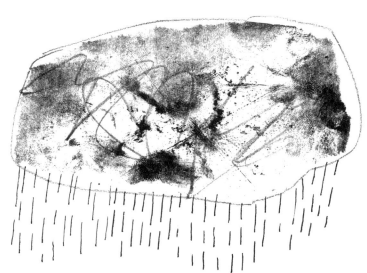

"Ladies + Gentlemen; the Rain has Stopped.
Play will Begin in 15 minutes."

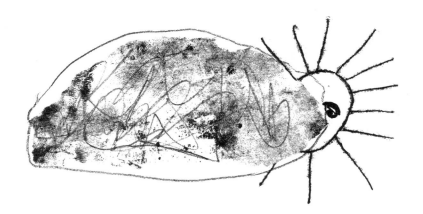

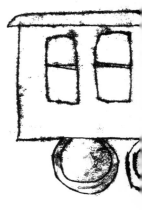

"And it's ANOTHER SIX! This is the BEST Innings I've EVER seen! What a Reward for the Patient Crowd—! Well Worth the Wait.."

AN ATTEMPT TO INFLUENCE THE UMPIRE WHEN RAIN STOPS PLAY~

←----Low Cloud & Precipitation----→
'Give over!'

BAD LIGHT

WE
SAY IT'S
BAD
LIGHT!

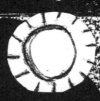

IDEAS FOR CRICKET MEMORABILA:

UNION JACK
BELLY BUTTON
SUN SHADE.

Historically-Stained M.C.C. Tie

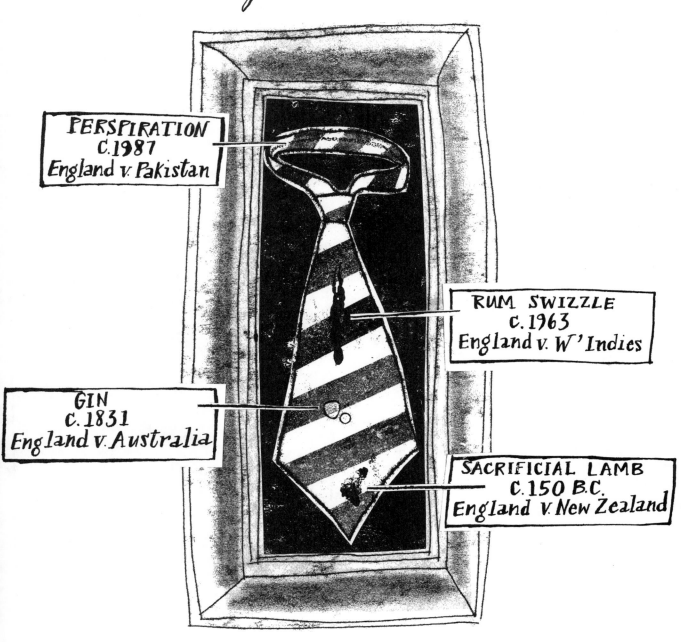

PERSPIRATION
C.1987
England v. Pakistan

RUM SWIZZLE
C.1963
England v. W'Indies

GIN
C.1831
England v. Australia

SACRIFICIAL LAMB
C.150 B.C.
England v. New Zealand

(Owner Unknown)

A SET OF 4 CIGARETTE CARDS:

#1
Dull, Effective Batsman
'SIR' GEOFFREY ECKESLIKE

1916-2056
't Joy Bells Rang in Pudsey'

#2
Demon Bowler
'OUR' TORRID TED HATETHWAITES

1866 - 1900
't 'Terror of t'World'

ALL-TIME FAVOURITES

#4
The Old Man
W. G.* GREAT

* What Girth

300 B.C. - 1915 A.D.
'Hammered Cricket Hearts to Destruction ♪

#3
Imperious Captain
LORD SMALL-TALKE

1860-1938
'A Christian and Prayerful Man ♪

The 'W.G. GRACE' RANGE...

FRIGHTEN THE OPPOSITION!
Life-Size 'W.G.' Cardboard Cut-Out-
Stands Convincingly at the Wicket.

LOOK AS SILLY AS W.G.!
One-Size-Fits-No-One
Cricket Cap.
(Genuine Facsimile)

INSTANT GIRTH!
Look Like W.G.-
Down-Padded
'Add-A-Belly'-
Goes Anywhere.

INDESTRUCTIBLE!
(Just Like W.G.)
'The Grace'-
Re-inforced
Athletic Support.
(Looks so Life-Like!)

SOME SOUVENIR PLATES—

ENGLAND vs. PAKISTAN

Winter Tour 1987

ASHES FLY TO AUSTRALIA

AUSTRALIA

with H.R.H. Prince of Wales

WHAT IF?...

The ACME Range of Products...

Umpires!
The ACME Remote-Control Sight-
Screen-Manipulator will allow
Members to continue sleeping in
Comfort.

The ACME Neo-Modernist-Tudor-Style Condo-Pavillion — A Combination of Tasteful Elegance & Old Country Nostalgia.